How to Run a Successful Accountancy Practice in Three Hours Per Week

Rudi Jansen

Table of Contents

Three Hours? 7

    The Best Business Model In The World? 9

    Complete The Questionnaire 12

A Clear Roadmap To Follow 15

    How Do We Build A New House? 15

    How Do I Build A Great Life? 17

    Step 1 – Idea 21

        Step 1, Part 1 — What do my family and I want for our personal lives? 21

        Step 1, Part 2 — What business(es) do I need to build that will give me that life? 22

    Step 2 – Onto Paper 24

    Step 3 — Building 25

    The Treadmill Model 26

    The Freedom Model 28

A+ Team 33

    Whose Chessboard Is It? 33

    Change Your Team Structure 34

    Outsourcing Or Offshoring 35

    Action Steps 35

A+ Systems 39

    Automate As Far As Possible. 40

    Are You Still A 'Doing' Organisation? 41

    Action Steps 41

A+ Growth 45

   1.   **Increasing The Number Of Clients**............................... 46

   2.   **Increasing Prices** 47

   3.   **Increasing The Average Number Of Services Each Client Purchases From You** 48

     Action Steps 48

A+ Leadership.. 51

     How Is Your Leadership? 51

     Vision 52

     Effective Delegation 52

Bringing It All Together 57

FAQ's.. 59

What Others Say 61

Next Steps 62

Want Some Help?.. 63

Additional Resources.. 64

Ready To Hang Up Your Boots? 65

THREE HOURS

Three Hours?

If you are reading this book, then you are probably a practice owner or a partner in an accountancy practice.

And like most practice owners, I am guessing that you are allocating a fair number of hours to your practice every week.
Or perhaps an unfair number of hours?
Or perhaps just far too many for the return you are getting back?

Like you I too run an accountancy practice.
With ten staff members and over four hundred clients.

But I run my accountancy practice in **three hours per week.**

In this book I set out for you step by step exactly how I do it.

You will find that nothing in this book is rocket science.
Because it is not the rocket science that achieves the dream.
It is the methodical, step-by-step implementation of the basics that achieves the dream!

This book was designed to be a quick read.
Grab a cup of your favourite brew.
Sit down.
Read.

By the time you take your last sip, you will have finished this book.

And you just may have a very different perspective on what is possible!

THE BEST
BUSINESS MODEL
IN THE WORLD

The Best Business Model In The World?

Accountancy practices come in all shapes and sizes, and yet accountancy is one of the best business models in the world.

I don't think there are many business models as brilliant as the model of a successful accountancy business.

Let's take a look at some of my friends:

Solicitor: I use them very rarely and only for the occasional big-ticket item.
Plumber: Hopefully I use them less than once in five years
Dentist: Hopefully I don't need to visit them more than once in ten years.
Piano teacher: Hard work for low money, selling time with some kids who don't really want to be there.
Scaffolder: I use them perhaps once in 15 years.

And on goes the list.

Most of those people are always on the hunt for new customers.

However, with my accountancy practice, what do we need to do?

Make sure we have the right team in place.
Make sure we have the right systems in place.

Find clients.

Treat them well.

And typically — unless they die — they will stay with us for 20+ years.
If we are really nice to them, they'll even tell their friends about us.

The biggest plus is that our clients trust us implicitly with their financial affairs. Which opens up a whole other world for us to help them in many other ways.

Now if that is not the ultimate "Recurring Revenue Plus" business model, then I don't know what is.

If we haven't met yet, in a nutshell a little bit about me:

1. I qualified as a chartered accountant in South Africa in 2002.
2. Around thirteen years ago, I left the accountancy world behind to become a top-class business coach, based in the UK.
3. For the last seven years, I have been working exclusively with accountants.
4. Following the successes of my clients, I decided to acquire a practice of my own to which I apply the exact same model that I have been teaching for the last seven years to help my clients set themselves free from the daily drudge of running their practices.
5. The results are predictably predictable.
6. Whilst I am still a full-time business coach for accountants, I work in my practice an average three hours per week.

For me, as a business coach to accountants, it is really interesting to notice how many various degrees there are within the model of 'accountancy practice'.

On the one extreme we have partners working 60+ hours per week with no life.
On the other extreme we have people like me working three hours per week in their practice.

And in between... there is anything imaginable.

The one practice owner I spoke with lives in France, with his practice in the UK. He is remotely set up to work from there. He flies in to spend one week per month in the UK. The rest he runs from France.

Another person has given up his office and runs a completely remote accountancy practice with his team of 28 people.

Another practice owner is spending two months of the year working remotely from Gran Canaria.

Some people have a net profit margin of 5%.
Others have a net profit margin of 65%.

Some have negative debtors.

Others have such high debtors that, if they collected it, they would have enough cash to put down a deposit on a brand-new Lear Jet.

Truly — anything is possible.

And what you choose to create — that is limited only by your imagination.

Why do my clients choose to have a specialist business coach who only focuses on accountants to guide them to success?

Because on the one hand knowing what is possible and on the other hand actually creating that possibility are two completely separate things!

Knowing that other people have already created a reality which you may want...

The questions you have to ask yourself are:

1. What do I have?
2. What do I want?
3. What is stopping me from creating what I really want?

In this book I share with you the same concepts I teach my clients and that I use in my own accountancy practice.

These concepts are based on principles.

When you warm metal up, it expands.
When you hold your hand in a flame, you burn.
Hamster wheels go round and round and round...

These are principles.

When you apply principles, you get predictable results.

This is exactly why I can take an accountancy practice, apply the same principles I have been teaching for years, and get predictable results.

Learn the principles.
Implement the principles.
And you can achieve the exact same predictable results.

There is NO reason for you to be stuck!

Complete The Questionnaire

To help you figure out which stumbling blocks are holding you back in your practice, download this questionnaire and complete it.

www.accoa.co.uk/3houraccountantworksheets

In less than five minutes you will have a full understanding of what is holding you back.

Those are the stumbling blocks that need to be removed so that you can truly live the life of your dreams.

TO RUN A SUCCESSFUL ACCOUNTANCY PRACTICE IN THREE HOURS PER WEEK, YOU NEED...

>———→

A CLEAR ROADMAP
TO FOLLOW

A Clear Roadmap To Follow

How Do We Build A New House?

If I wish to build a brand-new house from scratch, there are probably three big steps that we need to go through (and of course, hundreds of others along the way…).

Step 1 — IDEA: I need to get some idea in my head of what it is I am looking for.
Step 2 — ONTO PAPER: I need to go to an expert, the architect, to help pull this idea out of my head and put it onto paper.
Step 3 — BUILDING: Only now do we start putting the plan into action with financing, builders, etc.

If I was to ignore Step 1 — my future becomes a victim of the architect and the builder, they have no guidance on where to go or what to do…so they'll make something up that they think is okay.
If I was to ignore Step 2 — I'm putting all my hopes onto a builder being rather amazing and having a HUGE amount of experience to build without a drawing.
If I was to ignore Step 3 — it's all but a dream.

Steps 1, 2 and 3 are all important.
And — in that order.

How Do I Build A Great Life?

Let's follow some of the same principles we would be following for building our house.

Step 1 — IDEA

There are two key areas where we require clarity.
1. What do my family and I want for our personal lives?
2. What business(es) do I need to build to give me that life?

Step 2 — ONTO PAPER

Once we are clear on what an amazing personal life would look like and we have some ideas of the business we need to build to give us that life, then we put those ideas onto paper to help us clarify for ourselves, as well as for others, what it is we are intending on creating.

For our business, we write down a roadmap that we follow over the next three to ten years to help us get to our business destination.

Step 3 — BUILDING

Once we've got our ideas clearly written down on paper or in a spreadsheet, then we start following our roadmap step-by-step until we get to our destination.
Because Step 3 is so very important, this would also be the step where an accountability partner comes in very handy.

Knowing what you should be doing and then actively, step-by-step implementing it till it has actually been done are two very different concepts.

Most of us have a fair idea of what we should be doing. But then life happens – and interferes with the best-laid plans. The result is that somehow we continue running on this same old treadmill year-after-year with no real changes.
When you take your "I know what I should be doing" and to that you add an accountability partner who helps you figure out your roadmap for the next 10 years – and then, step-by-step holds you accountable to making it

happen, and if that person also brings with him a vast experience of working with others who have similar challenges to you... in this case, the chances that you will actually "do what you know you should be doing" increases ten-fold.

The person who says "I know what I should be doing, but I'm just too busy..." lives in a very different world to the person who says "I know what I should be doing – and I've done it."

The one is stuck on a never-ending Treadmill.
The other is enjoying a world of Freedom and Choice.

One of the major components that bridges between a World of the Treadmill and a World of Freedom and Choice is an Accountability Partner (especially one who actually knows what he's doing!).

Let's take a look at Step 1 and Step 2 in a bit more detail, because they are really important steps before we get to Step 3.
Getting clear on what exactly it is that you want to create in your personal life is the absolute first step.

It is really important that you do this one.

Most people never particularly bother with Steps 1 and Steps 2.
They simply jump straight into Step 3 and keep on Building, hoping for the best.

But for most of these people, they eventually reach a point where they realise that they are solidly stuck on the treadmill and have no idea on how to get off.

If you are running simply for the sake of running on the treadmill, soon enough you will find that you are not even bothering to think about how you could possibly get off it.

And yet, getting off the treadmill is absolutely, 100% predictably, possible.

WHAT IS YOUR
DREAM?

Step 1 – Idea

Step 1, Part 1 — What do my family and I want for our personal lives?

This is a very simple and straightforward process that will give you an immense amount of clarity!

Download the worksheet here:
www.accoa.co.uk/3houraccountantworksheets

The main points:
1. Make a listing of all the things you DO NOT WANT in your life
2. Write down the opposite of each item on that listing (therefore — This is what I DO want)
3. Turn those concepts into a story.

As an example.
1. What I don't want: I don't want to work 70 hours per week.
2. What I do want: I only work 20 hours per week.
3. Story 12 months from now: I am so excited. It's all come together and I've dramatically reduced my working hours. I am now only working an incredible 20 hours a week. I still can't believe it. Totally amazing!!! And I'm saying that with a big, happy and very grateful smile on my face. It is so great to spend the extra time with my family doing amazing things.

(That language is obviously mine. You will use your own language for this story.)

Number 1 helps you figure out what you don't want in your life.
Number 2 helps you clarify what you actually do want.
Number 3 turns this all into a story which you can easily turn into a video or a vision board to hold in your mind on a daily basis. Hold onto that image, no matter what, until it has come true. Sometimes that takes a few days, a few weeks, a few months, or occasionally even a few years...But eventually most things will become reality.

A real-world example of how this process helps clarify thinking:

I drive past the Range Rover showroom.
Do I get one, or don't I?

Could I afford one?
Yes, if I wanted.

But from the above process, I've identified that one of my personal goals is to be financially free and financially retired by the time I am 50 years old.

So, do I spend money on a monthly basis paying off the very nice Range Rover, or do I take that money to pay off a potential loan, which could be invested in property, another business or another accountancy practice?

Because I am clear on what my personal goal is, at this stage of the game I am choosing to say "no" to the Range Rover and "yes" to the good second-hand car that is 10 years old.

Get clear on what your personal goals are and you will become clear on what you say "yes" to and what you say "no" to.

Step 1, Part 2 — What business(es) do I need to build that will give me that life?

Only go to this step AFTER you've completed the previous step!

At this stage, we are very clear on what it is we want to create in our personal life.
We are clear what we will say yes to and what we will say no to.

We are still in the IDEA phase.

This is the dream phase.

This is the part where you dream about what you would love to have in the future from a business perspective.

The dream perspective is really important.

In the 1960's when John F. Kennedy announced to the world that within 10 years, America would land a man on the moon. At the time, it was completely impossible. The technology did not exist. And yet – within 10 years, it was done.

Elon Musk of Tesla and SpaceX is saying that we will colonise Mars... Right now that is not yet possible. It is only a dream. But I will bet my house that he will eventually pull this one off!

What is your dream?

Dreams originate from a different place to "Reality."

Just because your current reality is e.g. a turnover of £500k, who says that within 10 years you could not achieve £1mill. Or £2mill. Or £5mill. Or £20mill.

Never base your future on your past.

The question of "What business(es) do you need to build to give you the life you want?" is very much a "Dream" question.

If you could achieve anything, then what is your dream?

Because once you become clear on your Dream, the next step is "How in the world are we going to make that happen?"

Step 2 – Onto Paper

The next step is to create a Roadmap for your business on paper or a spreadsheet.

This is where you decide what your dream is for your business ten years from now.
What would be your absolute ideal?

In its simplest form, take the following steps:

Ten years from now, what is your turnover, your net profit, how many staff are working with you, how many hours are you working in an average week, how many weeks of holiday did you have in that year?

And what are the top five things that you need to focus on in Years 8, 9 and 10 to create that reality in Year 10?

After that, work it backwards...
To three years.
Again — what are the top five things you need to be focused on in Year 3 to create that reality?

Backwards again to one year from now?
And again — what are the top five things you need to be focused on during the next 12 months?

Backwards again to the next quarter.
What are the top three things that you need to be focused on during the next three months to move your business forwards?

At the end of this simple exercise, you will have for yourself and your team a very clear roadmap of where you are going and the actions you need to take over the next quarter to move you forwards on your roadmap.

Step 3 — Building

And now is the phase where you, one step at a time, build what you've created on your roadmap.

Remember that everything in your world is a project.

Every part of the machine that needs to be built is a mini project that needs planning, a project manager, and accountability to make it happen. Accountability from your team to you. Accountability from you to an accountability partner.

Build the small bits within the machine one step at a time and get it done. Just like Lego blocks.

And before you know it, because all the individual elements have been systematically put together, the whole machine will be systemised and built.

THE TREADMILL
MODEL

THE TREADMILL MODEL

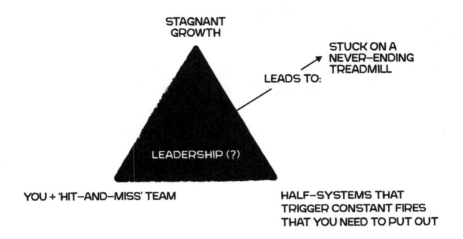

In the Treadmill Model you are essentially trading your life (your time) for money.

THE FREEDOM
MODEL

THE FREEDOM MODEL

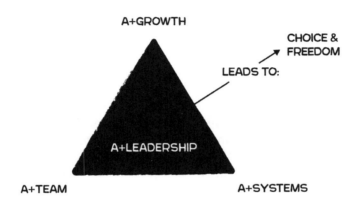

In The Freedom Model you have built a 'machine' that is making you money – whilst you then have the choice of what you want to do with your life and where you want to spend your time.

Either you've consciously created a model where you have:

A+ Team + A+ Systems + A+ Growth + A+ Leadership = Freedom

Or You:

Don't have   Don't have   Don't have   Don't have
  A+ Team + A+ Systems + A+ Growth +   A+ Leadership = Treadmill

Of the two options above, to build a business whereby you are only working three hours a week, the Freedom Model is non-negotiable.

The F1 racing car needs to be fine-tuned. Any one of the three corners of our triangle not in perfect condition will hold back our racing car — and that means that you are NOT working three hours or less a week in this business.

A choice that is yours to make is whether you choose to be at 'Enjoying a life of choice' or 'Enjoying a life of feeling like you've been imprisoned'.

Let's take a look at each of those corners of the triangle.

TO RUN A SUCCESSFUL ACCOUNTANCY PRACTICE IN THREE HOURS PER WEEK, YOU NEED...

>————————→

A+ TEAM

A+ Team

Let's take a look at possible symptoms of a non-A+ team:

1. You're working too many hours.
2. You're far too stretched.
3. You're frustrated with your team.
4. They are over-reliant on you and when things go wrong it falls back on to your shoulders.

Whose Chessboard Is It?

In the game of chess, which piece moves the least?
The king piece of course.

Now let's take a look at your real-world chess board.
Which piece moves the most?
I'm guessing that for most accountancy practices, the simple answer is You.
The king piece.

Can we agree that there is something wrong with that picture?
It is time to start shifting your real-world chess board so that the king piece moves much less and becomes much more strategic.

At the end of the day you are totally, 100% responsible for what chess pieces there are on your chess board and who is doing what.

If you are not happy with your chess board, then there is only one person on this planet who can change it.

And that is you!
Evaluate your current team members. Are they A+?

A very simple formula I designed for this is as follows:

A   +   A   =   A+

Attitude   +   Ability   =   A+

If you are going for the Olympic gold medal, then you need an A+ team behind you. Having a B or a C team is okay, but one thing is for sure — in that case you are absolutely guaranteed to NOT achieve the Olympic gold.

Building a business or an accountancy practice where you are only working three hours a week is absolutely, without a doubt, Olympic-gold medal status.

Which means that you having an A+ team behind you is non-negotiable.

The way to use the formula:

For each person in your team, rate them 0—10 for Attitude and Ability in their current role. Get the average of those two. If the average is eight or higher then you have an A+ team member.
Seven is a grey area. Six or less is no good.

An attitude rating of six or less is non-negotiable. Show them the door.
An ability of six or less means one of two things:
1. It is a possible training issue. That sits on your shoulders to ensure it is sorted.
2. We have a square peg in a round hole situation. The right person in the wrong role. Either move this person to the right role in your organisation or exit them.

Leadership is about doing the right thing, not the comfortable thing.

Change Your Team Structure

In order for you to do less, others need to do more.

Others could be people in your office, people outside your office, people on the other side of the planet, various tools, bits of software or automation.

A good question to ask yourself is: "If my hands were tied behind my back, how would I run this business? Who would be doing what?"

Always keep in mind the concept of a conveyor belt...where does it all start? How does it flow? For each stage of that flow, who is doing what, and who is responsible for what? How would that change if my hands were completely removed from the whole process?

Outsourcing Or Offshoring

The trend is that 'data capturing' or purely 'compliance work' is becoming more and more automated.

Anything that tends towards 'data capturing' you want to do as cheaply as possible in order to remain competitive and profitable.

For me, outsourcing or offshoring as part of your team who can do the 'data capturing' element of work for you, is a no-brainer. Yes, I know it takes roughly six to nine months to get these people trained up in your way. Yes, I know it is frustrating in Month 1 when you give them those rush jobs to complete and they fail miserably because they haven't yet been trained up in your way. Yes, I know it is frustrating to continually go back and constantly give feedback until they are trained but that is how people do get trained, right?

Stick with it, with the right partner, and six to nine months on, you will have an element of your business in place that is totally vital.

Action Steps

1. Decide in your head that you will ONLY have an A+ team.
2. Automate.
3. Actively move the wrong people on.
4. Actively push to get the right people in. Keep on and on and on until you only have A+ team members.
5. Be patient and get your outsourcing team trained up as part of your team.

TO RUN A SUCCESSFUL ACCOUNTANCY PRACTICE IN THREE HOURS PER WEEK, YOU NEED...

⤜————➤

A+ SYSTEMS

A+ Systems

If you are serious about building a business where you end up working three hours or less per week, then exactly as having an A+ team is non-negotiable, having A+ Systems throughout is non-negotiable.

If you feel that currently you do not have A+ systems, then fixing this is fairly simple.
It may not necessarily be very fast, but it is simple.

In order to fix your systems there are a few things that you need to be aware of:
1. Each system is a project.
2. Each project needs a project manager who is responsible and who you can hold accountable.
3. Each project needs a written down, bullet-pointed, high-level list of what needs doing in order to complete the project—normally around five to ten items with a time line for each item. Do a Google Search on 'Gantz Chart' to see an example.

Question to ask yourself: "Which system (or lack thereof) is creating the biggest headache right now in the business?"

And that is the system that you start working on first.

Once done, then you move on to the next system that is creating the next biggest headache.

You will find that the 80/20 rule[1] very much applies here. By getting a few of the major headache systems sorted, things will flow much better throughout your entire practice.

---

[1] Pareto's 80/20 rule essentially states that out of 100, roughly 80% is just stuff/busyness/waste. 20% makes the difference. For example – 20% of the roads in the country will carry 80% of the cars. 20% of kids in a school will cause 80% of the problems. 20% of your friends and family will give you 80% of your fun and joy. 20% of your clients will likely bring in 80% of your income. This rule applies everywhere. When you start looking for it, you will find it. The secret is to identify the 20% items that work & yield results and get more of that into your life, whilst at the same time you remove more and more of the 80% stuff that is simply eating up your time for very little return. This is one of the simple secrets to a very happy life.

Sit down with your team and come up with a list of the major headache systems.
Sort them in priority order, and you are all set to go.

Here are just a few examples:
1. Pricing system
2. Current debtors system
3. New client debtors system
4. New client onboarding system
5. Billing system
6. Workflow system
7. KPI system
8. Customer service system for A+/ A/ B/ C clients
9. Sales process
10. Automation

Pick one that will have the biggest impact.
Decide on a project manager (ideally not you as you are too busy with 101 other very important things).
Create a project plan for who does what by when.
Let the work begin.
Check in and hold people accountable.

Remember that with any project, you always want to build in milestones where you can touch base and get an update on the latest progress. There is no point starting a project today, if the next time you get an update is at the end of the timeline. It will be almost 100% guaranteed to be not-on-time or wrong.

Automate As Far As Possible.

Automation can save absolutely hours and hours of work.

Why not require that the majority of your clients use some form of cloud bookkeeping package — you may have to push hard to make it happen, but it will make your life much easier, especially if their bank details are directly imported.
A simple Google search will give you loads and loads of ideas of what can be automated.

NOT Automating is NOT an option.

Are You Still A 'Doing' Organisation?

Are you a 'Customer Service' organisation? Or a 'Doing' organisation?

The days of being a purely compliance-driven 'Doing' organisation are dead. If you remain like that, soon enough your organisation will be dead as well.

Which is why we are moving towards Automation. The 'Doing' no longer has much value in its own right. Competitors who can deliver the 'Doing' bit really cheaply are popping up all around you.

What your clients want is 'Customer Service'.

Set your organisation up to give much more Pro-Active Customer Service and you will go from strength to strength!

Action Steps

Automate:
1. With your team, research which parts you can automate and pick one.
2. Pick a project manager to make this happen.
3. Decide your project steps and a time line.
4. Implement step-by-step.
5. Check in and hold your project manager accountable on a weekly basis till it is completed.

Fix systems:
1. Decide which system (or lack of system) gives the most pain, irritation or grind at the moment.
2. Focus on getting this one system sorted once and for all.
3. Pick your project manager.
4. Decide your project steps and a time line.
5. Implement step-by-step.
6. Check in and hold your project manager accountable on a weekly basis till it is completed.
7. Pick your next most painful system, and repeat.

TO RUN A SUCCESSFUL ACCOUNTANCY PRACTICE IN THREE HOURS PER WEEK, YOU NEED...

➤━━━━➤

A+ GROWTH

A+ Growth

Yes, "A+ Growth" also refers to systems which underpins the growth.
But these systems are completely separate from your operational systems, which is why it has its own corner on the triangle.

The Business Stool
If we take a look at a stool.
It has three legs.

In order for the stool to stand upright all three legs need to be the same length.

Leg 1
Operational side of your business.
This is what we do.

Leg 2
Internal finance, HR and Admin.
This is the glue that holds it all together.

Leg 3
Growth, marketing and sales.
This leg brings in the work that we do.

If you were to rate each of these legs from 0—10, the perfect scenario is a stool that is steady.

For most accountancy practices, their stool falls over on Leg 3.

If yours truly is a business that is going places, then you need Leg 3 to be working properly.

We all know that there are three main ways to grow revenue
1. Increase number of clients *(Marketing)*
2. Increase prices *(Pricing)*
3. Increase the average number of services each client purchases from us *(Sales)*

1. Increasing The Number Of Clients

Marketing 101

How do we actually get marketing & lead generation right?

In simplified terms, there are two major steps:

If you imagine a spider's web.
1. Getting the basics is right in the centre of the spider's web.
2. Once the centre is solid, then we build the wider net to create the spider's web.

Basics:
1. Ensure your clients have a good experience by systemising your Customer Service System.
2. Ensure you have a good website.
3. You have a good LinkedIn presence.
4. You have systemised asking for referrals.
5. You have systemised your introducer relationships.
6. Possibly regular networking.

Those are items that a lot of us are doing in any case — but for most of us it happens very ad-hoc. You want to systemise this so we remove the ad-hoc bit.

Next step...when your prospects are lying awake at 2am in the morning, and they get onto Google to find solutions to their problems...that is when we want them to find you.

Build the wider spider's web:
This is mainly done through content marketing.
1. At least 1 blog post a week (and also re-posted onto social media)
2. White papers
3. Book(s) published
4. Downloadable fact sheets or checklists
5. Monthly Webinars
6. Quarterly Seminars
7. Paid advertising to drive interested parties towards downloading something or registering for a webinar or a seminar.

8. Telesales — when done correctly, this is an excellent resource for creating appointments. especially from prospects who have already engaged in your content.

Is any one of these methods on its own the absolute holy grail that will open the marketing tap for you?
On its own, not particularly.
But as a group that works together, they work like a spider's web...you're never exactly sure where the fly is going to get trapped, but you know it will happen! And the bigger that web, the better.

Are there more ways to do marketing and lead generation? Of course!
But if you get the abovementioned ticking like a machine, you will be a million miles ahead of the competition.

2. Increasing Prices

This is by far the quickest and easiest win to get in most practice.

One of the tools I share with my clients is a price survey I recently did with a group of my own clients. This tool has an anonymous listing of all the services these practices sell and how much they charge for it.

Knowing how to price optimally is a massive key.

As one of my clients recently said, "We've taken a long-standing client from paying £1,500 per year to £8,000 per year by having the correct system to price with."

Often the problem is not so much that we are not charging enough, but simply that we do not actually charge for the services we deliver.

The wrong mindset will cost you thousands in profit every single year!

3. Increasing The Average Number Of Services Each Client Purchases From You

If you are offering compliance services, then that is a great starting point.

It is great to come from the perspective that, ultimately, our clients are of course fully responsible for their financial world. But as their trusted advisors, we have a responsibility to help them be in control of their financial world as far as they possibly can.

Which means that we have a responsibility to sit our clients down, have a deep discussion about what they have in place and what is missing.
The missing bits... well, do we simply ignore that, or do we go out of our way to help them?

The concept above takes us far beyond purely compliance and tax work.

Very far.

To see a listing of over 50 other services you could offer clients, go to www.accoa.co.uk/3houraccountantworksheets

Action Steps

1. Get your pricing systems sorted.
2. Look at what other services you could assist clients with.
3. Then only start looking at marketing and lead generation...
    a. Get the basics systemised — one at a time.
    b. Once you are satisfied that your basics are in order and/or you have a real system built around each step, then it is time to move onto the more advanced systems.
    c. One at a time, put the more advanced systems in place — and always ensure it is a systematic process that is in place.

TO RUN A SUCCESSFUL ACCOUNTANCY PRACTICE IN THREE HOURS PER WEEK, YOU NEED...

A+ LEADERSHIP

A+ Leadership

How Is Your Leadership?

Great leadership can be taught.
Great leadership can be learnt.

If you were to rate yourself 0—10 for leadership, what number would you give yourself at this stage of the game?
The person who stands at the centre of an A+ team, A+ systems and A+ growth is at least an 8/10 on the leadership scale.

If you would not yet score yourself an 8/10, that is absolutely no problem. In the same way that you learn...

1. how to put together an A+ team, and
2. how to put together A+ systems, and
3. how to put together A+ growth,

...you learn how to get to a place where you can rank yourself an 8+/10 for leadership.

Everything I talk about in this book is teachable — and it is also learnable.

Whatever your score is at the moment, there is one big thing that you have going for you!
You would not have gotten to where you are today if you were not great at learning new things.

And that is why everything I talk about in this book is achievable.
Because it is learnable.

All you need is a real want, a real desire, to learn it and implement it.

If you bring that attitude to the table, then nothing stands in your way!

There is much to be said about leadership.
But two main keys are Vision and Delegation

Vision

The leader must have an ability to cast an exciting vision for the future.

Where are we going?

The way we discover this vision is by doing a strategic plan.
A roadmap.

Make a decision about where you want to be in the future, ten years from now, that's exciting and big enough.
Then paint that picture to your team and get them to buy into that vision.

Effective Delegation

Whenever you delegate ANYTHING, always use the Who-What-When Triangle.

1.   WHO:
ANYTHING you delegate needs ONE specific 'Who'.
Who is the person responsible?

This cannot be 'no-one', 'they', 'them', 'someone', 'everyone', 'the two of them'.
It requires one single name.

If two people are responsible for one project and the two of them are on the same level of seniority, then pick one of them to be the responsible person for the project. If that means you flip a coin, or alphabetically by first name...it doesn't matter how you decide. What is important is that you pick only one single name to be responsible — because this is the person you are going to hold accountable for this project.

2.   WHAT:
This is normally fairly straight forward.
This is the thing you want them to do.

3.   WHEN:
This is the area most people mess up on.

ALWAYS agree with the person by when they will get this done.

If you simply say, "John, will you bring me the audit file"…

Three weeks later when the audit file has not arrived yet, and you are going stark raving mad, you can't blame John. You had never agreed with him WHEN he will do this.

If you say, "John, will you bring me the audit file **by 2pm today** please" and John agrees with that, then you have brought in ALL three elements on the Who-What-When triangle. And you now have a tool with which to hold John accountable.

If he did agree to it and doesn't do it — then he has broken an agreement with you.

Always hold him accountable for the fact that he 'broke an agreement'. Don't bother holding him accountable for the fact that he didn't have the audit file on your desk at the time he agreed.

Never hold people accountable for 'things'.
Hold people accountable for 'the fact that you broke an agreement'.

Because there are 1,000 'things' that have great excuses.
But it takes only three broken agreements for you to no longer be a part of my team.

Good delegation requires three things:
1. Clear direction.
2. Milestones along the way for quick check-ins to ensure we're on the right track.
3. Holding people accountable.

Delegation is like a wheel that consists of two half-circles.
One half of the circle is 'Giving the task'.
The other half circle is 'Holding Accountable'.

Have you ever driven a car with half-wheels?
No — because it would be incredibly difficult.

Leadership is always about doing the right thing, not the comfortable thing.

Getting your A+ team sorted may not be comfortable, but it is the right thing to do.
Getting your A+ systems sorted may not be comfortable, but it is the right thing to do.
Getting your A+ growth sorted may not be comfortable, but it is the right thing to do.

Leadership is at the centre of our Freedom Triangle.

This is the mantle you are wearing.

Step up – and take the challenge.

Lead.

BRINGING IT ALL TOGETHER

Bringing It All Together

Step 1
Get clear on what you want for your personal life.
This gives you your 'why' for building your business.

Step 2
Build the next ten-year roadmap for your practice.

Step 3
Make some decisions around your A+ team and consider outsourcing.

Step 4
Automate as much as possible using available technology.

Step 5
Begin improving systems one at a time, starting with the biggest headaches first.

Step 6
Only now are you ready to really start focusing on growth and growth systems.

Step 7
The business will grow to a point where there are sufficient profits and cash flow to afford a management structure.

Step 8
Reduce your workload and time within the business — to three hours a week if you choose.

And that is how you (and I) can get to a place where we run a successful accountancy practice in three hours a week.

Building an accountancy practice that only needs three hours a week of your time is absolutely possible.

Others are doing it already.

I am too.

If you would like to explore what it might be like having an accountability partner to help you create this kind of reality, why not get in touch?

You can reach me at *rudi@accoa.co.uk.*

FAQ's

"But I am the brand. My clients only want to deal with me. How can I let go of that?"

This is always a big question. Others have already climbed this mountain, so this "letting go" is not at all impossible. And you will be surprised at how easily it actually is.

There is not a simple and straightforward answer to this question, other than stating that "It can absolutely be done!"

This is a process that will take time and in its simplest form is as follows:

1. You have to find your A+ team.
2. Identify your own "low-level" work and then systemise and allocate more of that onto your team's shoulders to free you up.
3. Allocate team members to work with certain of your clients.
4. Introduce your team to these clients and let these clients know that in order to improve customer service levels even further, going forwards this team member will be their first port of call.
5. Ensure that all queries that are aimed at you from these clients, you forward onto the team member and CC the client so that you "bounce" the email away from you to your team member to deal with.
6. This training of clients should on the whole be completed within a 12-month period.

"Can I do it?"

Who says you can't?

"But I don't want to build an empire?"

Building a 'machine' that takes you to freedom doesn't necessarily have to be massive.
Just big enough so you can afford the right team to run it mostly without you, and the right level of profitability is there for your requirements.

"But I'm in my sixties already?"

And?
It is all dependent upon your hunger and desire to make this happen.
Age has nothing to do with it at all.
Attitude and mindset does.

"But if I was only working three hours a week, I'd be bored!"

Yes, you could be.
Or you could spend your time on other things you love.
Like hobbies, holidays, family, friends, charity, building more businesses, making a real difference in the lives of other people, truly loving every day of your life!

"I don't have time for this!"

But you do have time to run like crazy on the treadmill?
It is completely your choice about what you want out of life.
At the end of the day, the only person who can make this happen — is you.

"Where can I find more details?"

This book has to a large extent been about the 'bigger picture'. If you want more specifics and more details then my other book, *The Highly Profitable Accountant,* has more detailed answers for you.

What Others Say

I consciously made a decision in this book NOT to have loads of testimonials and stories of clients. That you can find in my other book and on my website. The results when you go down a well-considered path which you and your team are held accountable to is totally predictable.

Recently one of my clients emailed me the following paragraph. In there, I hear the voice of hundreds of people that I've worked with over the years echoed over and over.

"I have joined many different accountancy type networks and found they all generally offer a large number of standard resources that are available on a "do it yourself" basis. These networks were not tailored to me or my business and they were very much selling stock intellectual property rather than something that was necessarily the particular assistance required for me and my business. Working with Rudi is the complete opposite. Although Rudi has a huge amount of helpful resources available for use, the process of working with Rudi is tailored to me and my business in a way I have not experienced with any other group or accountancy "pundit". In terms of building and improving my business, it is no exaggeration to say that I have achieved more during the 9 months I have been with Rudi than I achieved in the preceding 5 years. My business and I are achieving real traction with our ideas. Our ideas are no longer just ideas, they are becoming a reality. In terms of the accountancy business and the challenges practices face, it appears to me that Rudi has seen it all – and he has seen it time and time again. In any given situation he is able to offer practical advice and support – advice and support which has been proven to work before. Finally, in his own business, Rudi practices what he preaches. I would not hesitate in recommending any of my contemporaries wishing to improve their practices to work with him." - Antony Holdsworth

Next Steps

The knowledge in this book really can give you your freedom.

If that is what you want.

Of course, you could implement this by yourself. And if that is your choice, I honestly do wish you all the best of luck!

But if you feel you need further guidance...

If you've read this far and you're wondering how I might be able to help you get all these steps implemented, one step at a time as I have done with countless other practices, then there are some ideas on the following pages.

Want Some Help?

If you feel stuck and frustrated with where you are at, and you are absolutely serious about making changes, then why not arrange your complimentary, twenty-minute Practice Growth Session?

During the call you will:

- Discover the essential blueprint for growing *your* practice fast.

- Find out the #1 thing that's currently holding you back (and how to get around it).

- Identify the most powerful actions that will move you forward to the place you want to be.

The purpose of the Practice Growth Session is to troubleshoot your current situation and to determine if I can help you.

If I can help, then we'll arrange another call to figure out how. If I can't, then I'll try and point you in the right direction.

Please note — this call is only available for practices whose turnover is greater than £150,000 per annum.

If your current turnover is less than £150,000 per annum please see the following page for additional resources that could help you.

To book your complimentary, twenty-minute Practice Growth Session go to www.accoa.co.uk/session

Take that next step towards your own freedom.

Additional Resources

If you ever get stuck implementing the concepts in the book and need some extra help, I have a variety of additional resources to help you on your way:

Blog: every week I post short, actionable content to our blog in the form of videos, written articles and downloadable content. To find out more go to www.accoa.co.uk/blog

Online Training Session: in order to get the most out of the ideas and concepts in this book, you can also access a bonus online training. Register for free at www.accoa.co.uk/practice-growth-blueprint-training

Downloadable Guides & Cheatsheets: here are some of our most popular downloadable guides and cheatsheets that you can implement immediately to see results.

The Referrals Maximiser — The Three Step System That Signs A-Grade Clients
www.accoa.co.uk/referrals-maximiser

The Outsourcing Cheatsheet — The Three Step Process To Mastering Outsourcing
www.accoa.co.uk/outsourcing-cheatsheet

33 Ways to Increase Your Client Retention
www.accoa.co.uk/33-ways-to-increase-client-retention

The Highly Profitable Accountant — Order your free copy from
www.thehighlyprofitableaccountant.com

Ready To Hang Up Your Boots?

Perhaps you've read this book, but because of where you are in your life, you really can't be asked to make the changes — and you are ready to move onto the next phase of your life.

If you are thinking about it, or you are ready to sell your practice, the asset you've spent years of your life building, chances are very good that I might be able to connect you with someone who is looking to acquire your practice.

Get in touch with me.

I might be able to help you.

You can reach me at *rudi@accoa.co.uk*.